PRAISE FOR GORMAN POETRY

"Slightly lilting verse guides like a fast-moving laser through widely different topics, anchoring them with subtle verbal acrobatics into a pleasant and cohesive unit. *Poems of Life, Love, and the Meaning of Meaning* is a volume of self-help advice in a poetic format, a unique concept that delighted me... with a dry and witty take on life that flashed out like lightning... A highly individual book that will be enjoyed by minds that like to roam the galaxy in brief poetic installments."

—Sarah Scheele, *Readers' Favorite*

"A reflective experience that is both gentle in touch and penetrating in depth... The collection reminds me of the luminosity of a watercolor painting where bits of the underlayment shine through... Deceptively simple, the images the poems produce are thought-provoking without being heavy-handed or moralizing... The light-hearted approach to serious matters will appeal to many readers and makes this collection a perfect gift for friends and family who may just need a little prod toward healing and love."

—Kimberlee J. Benart, *Readers' Favorite*

Poems of Life, Love, & the Meaning of Meaning

—Gorman Poetry—

Copyright © 2018, 2024 Paul J. Gorman
All Rights Reserved

Year of the Book
135 Glen Avenue
Glen Rock, PA 17327

ISBN: 978-1-64649-410-1 (paperback)
ISBN: 978-1-64649-411-8 (ebook)

No part of this publication may be reproduced, distributed, or transmitted in any form or by any means, including photocopying, recording, or other electronic or mechanical methods, without the prior written permission of the author, except in the case of brief quotations embodied in critical reviews and certain other noncommercial uses permitted by copyright law.

TABLE OF CONTENTS

LIFE

- N/A 3
- Always with Me 4
- Something I Bring 5
- More Back to You 6
- Where You Could Be 7
- My Perfect Score 8
- Dear God 9
- Life Gives the Lesson 10
- The Right Thing 11
- Pause and Rewind 12
- That's What I Get 14
- I'll Win When I Lose 15
- Love in Each Moment 16
- Forever More 17
- It's Up to Me 18
- I Need to Be 20
- The Love that I Feel 21
- For Me to Be 22
- My Past Life Memory 23
- Myself I Met 24
- The Love I'd Get 26
- Love is the Source 27

In Love Instead 28
Love is Free 29
My Peace Within 30
Simple Close Moments 31
Raindrops... 32
Having Already Won... 33
Ego on Trial 34
The Heart Wall 35
What Could Have Been 36
Everything is Spinning.. 37
Our Little House... 38
Bumble Bee 39

LOVE

Hello 43
Your Eyes... 44
Dinner with You 45
Love Will Find Us... 46
Partners in Time 47
A Valentine 48
Tears 49
My Wish Come True 50
Sharing a Kiss...51
My Condition.. 52
As Near as Can Be 54
It Takes Two Hearts.. 55
The Perfect Cure... 56
Without a Sound 57
Our Emotional Affair 58
Your Voice 59
Why Can't We...60

Lovemaking Defined	61
Being with You	62
Another Place	63
The Love that We Know	64
Love is the Friend	65
In a Loving Pair	66
My Life Could Have Been	67
When You are With Me	68
Love Needs to Be	69
Our One Moment	70
A While Without End	71
Healing Two Hearts	72
Your Birthday	74
The Best of Friends	75
My Favorite Site	76
Your Love Inside	77
Having You With Me	78
Moments With You	79
Our Love Was Meant to Be	80
A Partner Like You	81
Loving You is Priceless	82
Our Love is Real	83
Ahead Looking Back	84
God's Love Song	85
To Love and Be Loved	86
\<untitled\>	87
The Love I Knew	88
My Love Will Stay	89
Your Laugh and Your Smile	90
Cabin in the Snow	91

THE MEANING OF MEANING

- Dorothy Gale 95
- I Am Each 98
- When I'm Being This 100
- Here and Now 102
- The Love that We Feel 103
- God, Me and You.. 104
- Forgiving is For Giving 105
- Just Me 106
- The Meaning of Life 108
- God Within... 110
- The Love that We Make 111
- Will Set Me Free... 112
- Until You Arrive 114
- To Be With You 116
- And Still Be With You 117
- God Needs Me.. 118
- Love in Me 119
- Our Light Within... 120
- Only Love Can Keep 122
- Heart and Soul 124
- You and Me 125
- I'll Know Myself 126
- I Wonder Why..127
- Each of Us... 128
- Here, When, and How 130
- I Love To Be.. 131

Afterword...133
Postscript..137

Love needs life, and life needs people loving life silently, open for its meaning.

—Spirit message

LIFE

N/A

Not applicable
   no need to apply
myself in life
   no need to try

she is dead
   the moon is fake
you expect me to believe
   that life is great

what does it take
   why ask why
does life create
   all it makes to die

Always With Me

Every day
   I pay the cost
of everything in life
   though it will be lost

and no longer mine
   gone in time
it can't be fair
   and I won't be fine

to lose my family
   pets and friends
and all that I love
   when each life ends

help me to see
   that their love will be
in my heart and soul
   and always with me

(keeping in mind
   life's irony
that these are the things
   I got for free)

SOMETHING I BRING

Beyond disappointed
   life passed me by
what did I hope for
   why did I try

I had every advantage
   sometimes needing a hand
people are busy
   I understand

what did I want
   need, or expect
a little love
   peace, and respect

precious commodities
   that don't cost a thing
are they something I find
   or something I bring

MORE BACK TO YOU

Life is marked
   by loss and pain
profit and gain
   not a zero-sum game

whatever you get
   start to give it away
you will be leaving
   but it will stay

there is one thing
   you can both leave and take
the love that you bring
   and the love that you make

give it away too
   and the more that you do
will not be lost
   but more back to you

WHERE YOU COULD BE

The nose went down
   heading into the ground
picking up speed
   then spinning around

the pilot announced
   he lost system control
above the screams
   the only sound

was my own voice
   asking where you could be
I won't survive
   and my dogs need me

I couldn't believe
   my life would end
in a few more moments
   and that was when

I awoke relieved
   my dogs near me
and asking again
   where you could be

MY PERFECT SCORE

There were some times
   brief moments past
when I reached perfection
   a perfect ass

when I didn't care
   or wouldn't try
wasn't aware
   and couldn't know why

so now I know
   and a whole lot more
including regret
   for my perfect score

DEAR GOD

God please help me
   in the time I have left
to live life again
   call it reality theft

to start anew
   just a few things to do
to be of service
   and to love life and you

now I'm ready
   here come people I knew
he had a good life
   the viewing is at 2.

LIFE GIVES THE LESSON

I blew it
  and I knew it
now I need
  to just get through it

my memories jaded
  and never faded
unwelcome guests
  in the life I created

my mind's not letting
  selective forgetting
and what I need
  to bypass regretting

why hang on
  to certain events
the past is gone
  if the mind relents

thanks for the reminders
  when not at my best
life gives the lesson
  after the test

THE RIGHT THING

It doesn't matter
   if you win
as long as you try
   then you will begin

to find the courage
   and resolve within
to do your best
   in everything

to not only try
   and not just anything
but to reach inside
   and do the right thing

PAUSE AND REWIND

I sometimes wonder
if I'm already dead
and now reviewing
what was in my head

what I did
and what I said
or didn't do
in the life I led

where I was weak
and when I was strong
how I was right
and why I was wrong

I learned a lot
    in hindsight it's true
now looking back
    as I review

I should have kept
    a peaceful mind
and not tried to get
    and not tried to find

anything except
    being aligned
with love and life
    and being kind

love in each moment
    was my lesson in time
now going forward
    I'll pause and rewind

THAT'S WHAT I GET

I was a young joker
   and sometimes a fool
trying to be funny
   wanting to be cool

I hurt her feelings
   and made her cry
I'm beyond being sorry
   now would rather die

I sometimes wish
   that I'd never met
anyone ever
   then I'd never get

embarrassed or upset
   humiliated and yet
it happened to me
   but I still regret

that I did it myself
   and cannot forget
so I live to forgive
   praying that's what I get

I'LL WIN WHEN I LOSE

What would it take
    for life to be great
a total success
    that I could create

there would not be
    any sadness or loss
with an excess of cash
    I'd be my own boss

and shouldn't it be
    a life without pain
no guilt or regret
    and only my gain

I'd pay to forget
    some memories I use
money can't buy
    the peace that I'd choose

so I'll let them go
    or change my views
my guilt and regret
    I'll win when I lose

LOVE IN EACH MOMENT

Every day
   there's another way
to choose what I do
   what I think and say

to feel and perceive
   to give and receive
and unto myself
   be truth or deceive

what is my truth
   but to heal and relieve
with love in each moment
   that's what I believe

FOREVER MORE

I changed my mind
 and did not fail
peaceful thoughts
  shall now prevail

my time is divided
  into weeks and days
now I've decided
  to change my ways

each day was composed
  of thoughts that I chose
feelings and judgments
  of things that I know

what if I'm wrong
  or choose to neglect
thoughts that aren't helpful
  using ones I select

they will be from love
  with peace at the core
mind and body contentment
  forever more

IT'S UP TO ME

Why would I get
    such a non-response
from people and life
    when it's not what I want

a disconnect
    no cause for effect
so let me guess
    it's my own defect

or maybe it's not
    and life is the cause
and I get what I got
    because life has its flaws

on ego planet
    where souls go for pain
in judgment and fear
    yet they want to remain

looking for love
    that they really need
fighting for peace
    following the lead

now I can see
    how love's guaranteed
but it's up to me
    to plant the seed

I NEED TO BE

Out of touch
   and out of time
out of luck
   and out of line

I cannot help
   to not be afraid
no price too much
   but the price I paid

to have lived in fear
   of what life could be
and lose the love
   I need to be

THE LOVE THAT I FEEL

There are some days
   I need a break
and want to opt out
   what does it take

to totally heal
   cut to the chase
skip the ordeal
   why need to wait

tell me what's real
   my lesson revealed
life unconcealed
   in the love that I feel

FOR ME TO BE

What if I could
   would, and I should
do anything at all
   something really good

I'd rid the world
   of judgment and fear
then violence and hate
   would disappear

selfishness and greed
   lies and abuse
are all in the past
   they'd have no use

we'd have what we need
   our minds would be freed
I'm starting right now
   and planting the seed

love and kindness
   is all I can see
there is nothing else
   for me to be

MY PAST LIFE MEMORY

As a young man
   I took to the sky
Fokker, DeHavilland
   and Grumman flying high

in the RAF
   for the King and Queen
March '44
   is the last I was seen

from schoolboy to war
   the first group to Berlin
dropping our bombs
   no choice but to win

our squadron returning
   near the border of France
a mid-air collision
   didn't stand a chance

an end to that life
   I died at the scene
my past life memory
   dead at 18

MYSELF I MET

Three hundred thousand
   die every day
and if they could speak
   what would they say

I was ready to go
   or wished I could stay
or to have lived my life
   in my own way

the show's not over
   just my part in the play
I've gone with God
   one heartbeat away

I am almost at peace
    but to my dismay
I was the piper
    I did not pay

with due respect
    love and attention
what I'd expect
    and not to mention

I gave it to others
    and to my pet
now I'm dead
    with one regret

not loving myself
    while alive and yet
when I met God
    it's myself I met

THE LOVE I'D GET

What if I
    was totally poor
no source of income
    and was never sure

when I would eat
    be warm and secure
if I'd stay well
    or even endure

would I find
    life unkind
feeling abandoned
    in my mind

or could I gather
    the things I need
food and water
    and a place to sleep

with the love of God
    and a homeless pet
there is no limit
    to the love I'd get

LOVE IS THE SOURCE

I don't believe
   in having beliefs
unless they will lead
   to my inner peace

that's deep inside
   behind the fear
beyond what I think
   what I see and hear

around the judgment
   past guilt and shame
what others want
   self doubt and blame

life is a gift
   set on a peaceful course
for healing itself
   and love is the source

IN LOVE INSTEAD

Again I feel
   as if I'm dead
and now reviewing
   the life I've led

the best intentions
   were in my head
and in my heart
   not what I said

please forgive me
   so I can forgive myself
and continue to live
   in love instead

LOVE IS FREE

How could it be
   that love is free
as well as the air
   and fruit from a tree

what about peace
   forgiveness and light
a baby's smile
   and the stars at night

we own them all
   but pay for regret
judgment and shame
   is our only debt

pay it all off
   with our endless supply
of forgiveness and love
   it's free and that's why

MY PEACE WITHIN

There is a place
   of peace inside
where I can go
   and sometimes hide

from fear and regret
   to briefly forget
the devils and clowns
   I've always met

in my life
   and in my mind
ego reflections
   a kind unkind

never alone
   inside my shell
life rages on
   and all is well

stay with me
   our outside in
you are my peace
   my peace within

SIMPLE CLOSE MOMENTS

What is life
    but a time to remember
simple close moments
   of our time together

at the end
   when life slips away
what will be left
   what more to say

not the work
   and not the things
but simple close moments
   their healing love brings

looking back
   giving me peace
our simple close moments
   my life I release

RAINDROPS

Raindrops are falling
 and are never still
the cycle of life
 that we fulfill

tiny drops
 one by one
then as a stream
 our purpose begun

to gently flow
 and find our way
to rivers and lakes
 and oceans away

one sea body
 from which we came
then back to the clouds
 we are one and the same

HAVING ALREADY WON

How would it feel
    apart from the divine
in a deal that seems real
    and a game only mine

I'd create an ego
    and project it out
looking for lack
    within and without

when I realize
    that there's only one
the rules of the game
    come totally undone

why would the game
    have ever begun
what could I win
    having already won

EGO ON TRIAL

You stand accused
   of disturbing the peace
and making false claims
   your lies never cease

creating division
   separation and pain
you show no remorse
   finding others to blame

you then covered up
   with serial evasions
the unloving offenses
   on countless occasions

I don't judge or condemn
   that was your game
in the light of truth
   is where you will remain

THE HEART WALL

Totally unconscious
   and for my own good
I built a heart wall
   with whatever I could

disappointment and despair
   paid for and installed
sadness and hurt
   I used it all

made out of pain
   is a barbed wire fence
to top it off
   for my heart's defense

the heart is not free
   and needs protection
behind a wall
   to avoid detection

not always visible
   and ten feet tall
when you can see it
   your wall will fall

WHAT COULD HAVE BEEN

He's gone without knowing
    what could have been
his chance of a lifetime
    to love from within

your heart could have been
    his favorite art
above all there is
    it's priceless and his

your dreams could have been
    his favorite game
where you always win
    and no two the same

your thoughts could have been
    his favorite edition
the first book of wisdom
    in perfect condition

his life was without
    and not from within
to have and to hold
    what could have been

EVERYTHING IS SPINNING

Is everything spinning
   or is it just me
my chakras, the planet
   the whole galaxy

whirlpools and twisters
   wheels and fans
washers and dryers
   and Saturn's bands

now I'm dizzy
   spiraling down
electrons in orbit
   the clock spins around

stay with me
   so I don't turn and roll
or pull the pin
   let me spin out of control

OUR LITTLE HOUSE

I don't want bills
   a lawn or big house
but a life that's filled
   with love and my spouse

we're always at home
   wherever we roam
collecting treasures
   in our hearts alone

simple pleasures
   and joyful giving
we're learning a life
   not earning a living

our time together
   is much better spent
enjoying each moment
   than paying the rent

no house can hold
   all that we own
the love in our hearts
   and the joys we have known

BUMBLE BEE

Bumble Bee
   tell me why
don't you know
   you're not supposed to fly

come back down
   keep your feet on the ground
don't you know
   you're too big around

this doesn't look good
   you could totally fail
or not be good enough
   you need a tail

I'm only trying to help
   you're a Bumble Bee
you're not going to believe
   so wait for me

LOVE

HELLO

I promise I won't
  love you too much
care too deeply
  or try to touch

your heart and soul
  a lover's role
as you touched mine
  though I've lost control

and can't let go
  or ever unknow
love that's forever
  and ever, Hello

YOUR EYES

If I could see
   your eyes seeing me
I would not move
   and just want to be

in your look
   and in your sight
into your retinas
   on waves of light

then to your brain
   and your DNA
inside forever
   is where I will stay

now shut them tight
   and see inside
behind your eyes
   where love resides

DINNER WITH YOU

Dinner with you
   I'll meet with the crew
to discuss our order
  and the best they offer

we'll talk about things
  that physical life brings
our joyful treasures
  and physical pleasures

when the server asks
  is there anything more
I'll let him know
  I'll take you to go!

LOVE WILL FIND US

If our eyes met
   we'd never forget
our moment of knowing
   and the feeling we'd get

seeing each other
   and to recognize
one hundred lifetimes
   in each other's eyes

here and now
   as then before
what are we doing
   what is it for

each time we would know
   and our lives are to show
that love will find us
   wherever we go

PARTNERS IN TIME

If I could pick
  a time and place
to be together
  and see your face

I'd choose them all
  leaving none
partners in time
  in every one

A VALENTINE

A Valentine
  a glass of wine
and a day with you
  my things to do

it's at the top
  of my list
and every day
  the one I missed

when is the day
  that I can say
now we're together
  and together we'll stay

TEARS

I kiss your tears
    healing each one
with hurt removed
    and sorrow undone

they just want
    to run down your face
and kiss your lips
    to take my place

MY WISH COME TRUE

A trillion thoughts
   and a million dreams
an entire lifetime
   of reality scenes

they come and go
   the joys and pains
of all my hopes
   one wish remains

to be with you
   and be with you
my million dreams
   my wish come true

SHARING A KISS

I kissed your lips
   and in an instant
eternal particles
   no longer distant

all the dimensions
   and all of our layers
held in suspension
   for just two players

time is gone
   letting in bliss
sharing with you
   sharing a kiss

MY CONDITION

I have an illness
   that comes in the stillness
it's more an affliction
   maybe an addiction

I got it from you
   but it's not contagious
a quick progression
   that came in stages

left untreated
   symptoms repeated
no one's immune
   or love depleted

it affects the brain
    body and behavior
heart and arteries
    and you are my savior

from a terminal condition
    I could recover
to spontaneous remission
    if you were my lover

I need to get well
    so help me please
I can't heal myself
    if love's a disease

AS NEAR AS CAN BE

I'll take a plane,
   a boat and a train
just to meet you
   I'll walk in the rain

to be where you are
   no matter how far
I've already started
   I'm in the car

no GPS
   no map or directions
no rear view mirror
   just my intentions

to be with you
   together as 'we'
on the trip of a lifetime
   as near as can be

IT TAKES TWO HEARTS

I ask myself
   why haven't we met
not gotten together
   not once and not yet

I would love
   to be with you
wherever you are
   in a pair of two

two ears, two eyes
   is what we get
but it takes two hearts
   for an unbroken set

THE PERFECT CURE

I need a prescription
   that you can fill
for my description
   of love fulfilled

it heals the heart
   and lessens the pain
it doubles the pleasure
   and joy in the brain

it's not a pill
   that they can sell
and just one dose
   will make you well

raw and organic
   and totally pure
they cannot patent
   the perfect cure

WITHOUT A SOUND

A weekend at home
   to be alone
with no distractions
   no chores or phone

a mini death
   a silence to own
a quiet mind
   a true love poem

written for you
   as if you are here
what I feel
   is what I hear

love is quiet
   in total surround
silence is broken
   without a sound

OUR EMOTIONAL AFFAIR

Our emotional affair
    and hearts laid bare
beating together
    an identical pair

don't they know
    our minds won't dare
to follow our hearts
    or just not care?

YOUR VOICE

Yours is the voice
   I want to hear
whispering
  in my ear

make the sound
   of love surround
around the quiet
   two heartbeats pound

a rhythm and tone
   words never alone
your voice that captures
   life's fleeting raptures

WHY CAN'T WE

Why can't we
   make love today
and be together
   in every way

with nothing to lose
   and nothing to gain
our life in the moment
   that's forgotten the pain

why can't we
   live by a beach
past the end of the road
   and out of reach

we'll have all that we wanted
   or ever need
love and each other
   why can't we

LOVEMAKING DEFINED

If we were together
 I don't know whether
we would make love
 or love would make me

whole and alive
 and totally complete
to love your body
 from your head to your feet

and to love your mind
 generous and kind
life's expression
 of love aligned

and to love your spirit
 being one with mine
lovemaking together
 lovemaking defined

BEING WITH YOU

What did I do
    to make me lose
going through life
    missing my cues

as I review
    significant moves
going through life
    when having to choose

I'd trade them all
    for one that's new
for going through life
    being with you

Another Place

I know what I want
   and what I will do
just to run away
   and be with you

we'll go past beyond
   and further than far
and keep on going
   to a place that we are

together and free
   to love and let be
two beings together
   just you and just me

we'll be far away
   and past what's expected
to another place
   that our dreams selected

there I'll see in your face
   and I'll know in my heart
that I had what I wanted
   right from the start

THE LOVE THAT WE KNOW

If we don't meet
   it will be okay
we'll be apart
   and stay this way

until time collapses
   and space disappears
taking our bodies
   our hopes and our fears

we will still be here
   reunited as one
there's nowhere to go
   with separation undone

the two illusions
   that keep us apart
space must have limits
   and time has to start

so they cannot be real
   except as a show
that we're not what we think
   but the love that we know

LOVE IS THE FRIEND

I wanted a love
 of my own
to be my friend
 and not be alone

earlier attempts
 had totally failed
they could not last
 my life derailed

I am not sad
 for the time that's lost
nor for the price
 that wisdom cost

now I'm alone
 my plans fell through
love is the friend
 I have in you

IN A LOVING PAIR

I tried to connect
 with people I'd met
sharing my thoughts
 my feelings, and yet

they did not care
 or indifference I'd get
it wasted my time
 and made me regret

why did I share
 if it wasn't fair
I want to be with you
 in a loving pair

MY LIFE COULD HAVE BEEN

I'd like to go back
   and begin life again
to earlier in time
   I don't know when

I got off track
   and out of sync
when I was confused
   and had to think

not hearing myself
   when making choices
my truth above
   the noise and voices

if you were there
   I would have seen
the beauty and truth
   my life could have been

WHEN YOU ARE WITH ME

All that I want
  is to be with you
no place to go
  nothing to do

we'll sit and talk
  and have some tea
then go for a walk
  at a quarter of three

or quarter till four
  no difference to me
I'll have all that I wanted
  when you are with me

LOVE NEEDS TO BE

I can love
 your entire being
by knowing and feeling
 hearing and seeing

without my eyes
 my ears and mind
love transcending
 our space and time

inward and outward
 the love at our core
is endlessly flowing
 forever and more

flowing and free
 love needs to be
life's reason for being
 inside you and me

OUR ONE MOMENT

I don't know whether
  it would be better
if we were together
    for a day or forever

each of our moments
    all in a row
or only one great one
    to love, heal and know

A WHILE WITHOUT END

Let me love you
 for just a while
to feel your warmth
 and see your smile

and a while longer
 to be with you
add some time again
 a while or two

while after while
 the time that we spend
let me love you
 for a while without end

HEALING TWO HEARTS

What if life
   is a vast construction
appearing real
  like a movie production

and we choose the props
   the cast and the crew
filming has started
   and each day is new

healing scenes
   some adventure and fun
but the major theme
   is how two become one

two lives, two minds
    that fall in love
one spirit, one purpose
    they rise above

sub-plots and bad actors
    and no other factors
have as much meaning
    as the love they are feeling

next is the part
    where the lovers meet
Healing Two Hearts
    co-starring you and me

YOUR BIRTHDAY

You never die
   so were never born
just incarnated
   into human form

a life of beauty
   love and grace
just the one
   to brighten this place

your life's a treasure
   a healing presence
by every measure
   it's your life essence

if you could see
   yourself through me
you'd see a woman
   no other could be

sweet and kind
   you help me through
I have no gift
   the gift is you

THE BEST OF FRIENDS

I won't care
   when I die
what is true
   and what's a lie

I'll be done
   but had to try
to be with you
   and I'll know why

love is truth
   and life a charade
we traveled through
   a love parade

now it's clear
   as the marching ends
we knew love
   as the best of friends

MY FAVORITE SITE

You are my website
   my group and my thread
my little tweet
   and blog in my head

love is our link
   and your user name
downloading files
   from your domain

every post
   chat and text
securely connected
   to what I like best

our meetups in space
   a healing place
the mind and heart
   cannot erase

my favorite site
   on our inner net
my memory card
   will never forget

YOUR LOVE INSIDE

Inside your heart
   and inside your mind
is where to start
    and where to find

the love of life
    loving blind
life's expression
    and love of mine

beautiful woman
    you cannot hide
what shows all over
    your love inside

HAVING YOU WITH ME

I want to go back
   and live life again
with you as my lover
   my wife and my friend

I got my wish
   but found you too late
now we're much older
   our time couldn't wait

living in hindsight
   and sad to regret
with trapped emotions
   I want to forget

my life should have been
   what I wanted it to be
loving and free
   having you with me

MOMENTS WITH YOU

How could life
   be a success
by any measure
   without you unless

success has no joy
   no love to express
a world of just one
   no more and no less

or success has no feeling
   and nothing to give
no reason for healing
   its conditions to live

my success is measured
   not in leisure or pleasure
but in moments with you
   that I forever treasure

OUR LOVE WAS MEANT TO BE

Do I have fear
   of intimacy
to totally share
   between a partner and me

and am I afraid
   after what I paid
in relationships past
   when pain outweighed

and hopes were dashed
   dreams were crushed
love was lost
   with connection and trust

what wasn't there
   what didn't I see
you're the one I need
   our love was meant to be

A PARTNER LIKE YOU

Why would I feel
    afraid to be alone
single and free
    and on my own

I understand
    it's my biggest fear
to be living solo
    year after year

I'd been there before
    but couldn't take more
down for the count
    and out on the floor

hope got a beating
    romance got bashed
my self esteem
    was totally trashed

what can I do
    besides start anew
what I wanted in life
    was a partner like you

LOVING YOU IS PRICELESS

The best investment
    that I can make
starting right now
    it's never too late

is to be with you
    spending time together
dividends and interest
    compounding forever

I'll reap what I sow
    and know what the price is
on profits that grow
    loving you is priceless

OUR LOVE IS REAL

What I need
   is peace of mind
my life requires
  that I find

a quiet state
   no mental chatter
mostly words
   that do not matter

so instead
   I think of you
imagining things
   that we could do

then I feel
   as my mind heals
peace of mind
   that our love is real

AHEAD LOOKING BACK

If I went ahead
  and looked back at now
to see your life
  and to tell you how

your loving thoughts
  are all that is real
they are what you are
  and are what you feel

they'll make your day
  your week and your year
one after the other
  until you are here

ahead looking back
  at what I can see
kindness and love
  from eternity

GOD'S LOVE SONG

What people need
   I looked it up
besides food and shelter
   is only love

where can we find
   the love we require
and also fulfill
   our heart's desire

go inside
   where it's totally still
at your source of God
   and stay until

you know real peace
   fear and doubts release
you feel God's love
   and self-love increase

there it will be
   it was you all along
the love that you sought
   you are God's love song

TO LOVE AND BE LOVED

I don't need memories
 I don't need friends
I don't need time
 or money to spend

I just need you
 for my heart to mend
to love and be loved
 until the end

<UNTITLED>

Born too young
   or lived too long
everything's right
   and something's wrong

why fit in
   and try to belong
always in life
   needing to be strong

I'll take a rest
   I did my best
and don't want more
   just less unless

the one thing left
   I do not lose
is the love in life
   I have with you

THE LOVE I KNEW

I always expect
   to live a long time
in pretty good health
     until a final decline

what will happen
     will I be scared
or ready to go
     and fully prepared

will you be there
     to see me through
when I say goodbye
     to the love I knew

MY LOVE WILL STAY

What if I learned
    I had a fatal disease
a short time to live
    just a matter of weeks

I'd call you up
    and let you know
no, better keep quiet
    not let it show

then I'd sit down
    and write you a note
to tell you goodbye
    that I have to go

try not to cry
    when I slip away
our love will live on
    after that day

and past my time
    in another way
beyond my life
    my love will stay

YOUR LAUGH AND YOUR SMILE

You lifted my spirits
  with your laugh and your smile
though I only knew you
  for a little while

then lost touch
  for 30 years
and news of your death
  brought me to tears

what did you do
  to make me so sad
my memories are joyful
  of the times that we had

to lose an old friend
  for your life to end
the world will be less
  and our gift was when

there was only love
  that was your style
I'll always remember
  your laugh and your smile

CABIN IN THE SNOW

Heart to heart
   and toe to toe
making love
   in the fire's glow

burning embers
   the heart remembers
fears that melted
   long ago

turning to streams
   watering dreams
of flowers in spring
   and the message they bring

that life is love
   and love is a flow
keeping us warm
   when the cold winds blow

it's safe inside
   where you will know
I am the cabin
   in the snow

THE MEANING OF MEANING

DOROTHY GALE

The witch was her ego
   out of control
bent on destroying
   the truth she held close

her truth was Toto
   the scarecrow her mind
to help her get home
   which they set out to find

discovering her heart
   gentle and kind
corroded and stuck
   having lost its shine

out came her courage
   which admitted through tears
after chasing her truth
   that it had only fears

together they went off
   and followed her thoughts
all little people
   certain she's lost

to find a higher power
    the Wizard of Oz
exposed as a fraud
    by her truth as a dog

apples and poppies
    and ego demands
an ego determined
    to sabotage their plans

her higher self Glenda
    softly pointed out
that the heart-shaped slippers
    are what she's raging about

don't give them up
    to the ego's control
stand in your power
    by connecting your soles

but flying monkeys
    of guilt and regret
the ego sent out
    to get her and her pet

they tore up her mind
    and damaged her heart
couldn't hold her truth
    and let her courage depart

Dorothy was doomed
    and scheduled to die
to lose her power
    and didn't know why

but her courage got behind
    as her mind made a plan
how to save Dorothy
    while the hourglass ran

diminished by water
    as life in the flow
the ego was finished
    no one missed it go

Dorothy got home
    but was surprised to see
that she had never left
    and her life was a dream

this is the tale
    of her crossing the veil
the life and the death
    of Dorothy Gale

I AM EACH

I used to believe
    we get what we deserve
until each time
    life throws us a curve

I used to buy in
    to the Law of Attraction
thoughts making things
    a mind action reaction

I used to think
    that life gives us chances
for forgiveness lessons
    so our soul advances

now I don't know
    or why it is so
if we're a part of God
    though a tiny fraction

but that can't be
    it's not so because
to divide All that is
    makes it All that was

the only answer
    that makes sense to me
is that I am the Creator
    making a dream to see

like soap needing dirt
    so it can clean
with love and healing
    in every scene

I'm out of context
    and don't like to be
a fish out of water
    in life's duality

so I'm opting out
    and don't want a fake dream
I'll be myself
    with no self or esteem

I am only love
    and have only peace
I will not judge
    that's all I can teach

to be at my core
    and there I will reach
flowing stillness of Source
    I am All, and I am Each

WHEN I'M BEING THIS

Now I'm sorry
   and I take that back
I am not at the Source
   just a spiritual hack

I need a drink
   after that personal attack
why would I create
   so much lack

of what I want
   and really need
love and peace
   in harmony

now here's a twist
   it may not exist
many have searched
   and many have missed

but I continue on
   and cannot resist
searching for them
   until I cease and desist

but they are only inside
   love and peacefulness
and I'll know the Source
   when I'm being this

HERE AND NOW

If time and space
   are not even real
vast constructions
   designed to reveal

that here and now
   is where we allow
love in each moment
   to show us how

love is timeless
   and needs no space
our inner being
   now here in place

in our hearts
   and in what we feel
we're here and now
   and how life heals

THE LOVE THAT WE FEEL

Life's an illusion
   and all a deception
a trick of the mind
   on our perception

it comes and goes
   so cannot be real
a temporary illusion
   for us to heal

what our minds conceal
   in our own creation
that feels the pain
   of separation

to think we're apart
   from All that is
the contradiction
   our mind forgives

healing itself
   as we reveal
love eternal
   in the love that we feel

GOD, ME AND YOU

In 100 years
   we'll all be gone
except for a few
   still hanging on

where will we go
   from where did we come
how did it start
   and when is it done

I understand
   that life's an idea
putting in motion
   the separation of one

which cannot be divided
   or ever undone
given time and space
   as a place to run

and all that we need
   for what we choose to do
remembering the oneness
   of God, me and you

FORGIVING IS FOR GIVING

I go inside
   where I can hide
but am not alone
   until I decide

that guilt and regret
   the demons I met
are no longer welcome
   so I try to forget

but I need to forgive
   them one by one
for myself and others
   until I am done

healing myself
   and the world I project
forgiving is for giving
   and the gift I will get

JUST ME

If I was God
   what could I do
to know myself
   so my love comes through

what could I be
   that's not already me
I'd make a mirror
   an illusion to see

in my own image
   a reflection it's true
before there was one
   now there are two

I'll give it a life
    free will and some time
to learn of its source
    which is really just mine

in my creation
    for things to exist
there is an equal
    and opposite list

dark without light
    cold without heat
love without fear
    is where we will meet

that is my dream
    for my illusion to see
out of the mirror
    no illusion, just me

THE MEANING OF LIFE

I still don't know
   the meaning of life
why there is hardship
   suffering or strife

it can't be an illusion
   or an attraction of lack
or manifestations
   streaming back to back

maybe it means
   something different to each
what we like or need
   what we can learn or teach

what gives us purpose
   or makes us aware
developing our gifts
   that we can share

to lessen the pains
   in need of repair
life isn't perfect
   or totally fair

maybe that's it
   and there is no why
that the meaning of life
   is just that we try

GOD WITHIN

Where was God
    some people ask
with the victims
    and in healer's tasks

three sides of a coin
    that we receive and give
an outer edge
    between evil and live

a very fine line
    through stillness within
where all sides meet
    God ends and begins

it's up to you
    in the coin you use
God within
    the side you choose

THE LOVE THAT WE MAKE

I'm healing myself
   from being alive
for trying to win
   just wanting to thrive

why did I choose
   the human race
for my soul advancement
   in time and space

then bought into fear
   guilt and shame
and judgment of others
   that are all the same

the pain feels real
   from living that lie
and I need to heal
   before I die

what does it take
   in the lives we create
forgiveness and peace
   from the love that we make

WILL SET ME FREE

I cannot shake
  the memories
of how I had hurt
  in varying degrees

not hurting others
  or other hurting me
but in hurting myself
  now painful times three

and I'm making it worse
  into an eternal curse
replaying the guilts
  by chapter and verse

I want to go back
    to redo them again
rehearse them first
    in reverse to when

I can think and choose
    what will be the best
and not misuse
    the truth in jest

to later regret
    what I had said
guilt zombies undead
eating joy in my head

now that I see
    what's ailing me
self love and forgiveness
    will set me free

UNTIL YOU ARRIVE

What if I lived
   on the planet alone
one world for each
   and to each his own

no other people
   no cars or phone
from what I could find
   I would build a home

no language or money
   no country or borders
no wisdom or books
   no lies or orders

I would never be late
    or have payments to make
would not be important
    or need to fake

having no guilt
    and no reason for shame
with little to gain
    and no place for blame

my motivation
    would be to survive
to work with nature
    and to stay alive

I'd have no purpose
    or reason to thrive
and would not know love
    until you arrive

TO BE WITH YOU

I don't care
   when I will go
it's only where
   that I would like to know

and I understand
   there's no time or space
and the thoughts I make
   will then create

in an instant
   whatever I think
to manifest
   all in a blink

time and space
   then I suppose
are limitations
   self imposed

so what I'll do
   when my life is through
is make more time and space
   to be with you

And Still Be With You

God, I forgive you
    for playing a part
or creating the conditions
    for me to depart

and end up here
    year after year
in a world of potential
    limitations and fear

I gave it my all
    forgave them all
knew temptation
    and heard my call

lived a life
    and stood up tall
spoke my truth
    and took the fall

God, please tell me
    what can I do
to be in this life
    and still be with you

GOD NEEDS ME

God needs me
   or would never feel
fear and doubt
   or pain that's real

poor being
   of one dimension
only love
   no real comprehension

of guilt or shame
   mistakes or blame
or forgiving itself
   that's why I came

so now I know
   God is not complete
without my experience
   God needs me

LOVE IN ME

I was wrong
 and God can't need
because love is all
 and free to be

a song can't sing
 and a book can't read
water can't drink
 and air can't breathe

God is love
 and now I can see
life needs God's healing
 from love in me

OUR LIGHT WITHIN

I look at myself
   and have to laugh
so serious about life
    times one and a half

to come out of a woman
    when I was nine months old
on the day I was born
    or so I was told

what if I go back
    six hundred thousand months
or fifty thousand years
    to birth number one

and who was she
    the mother to be
there must be a father
    but how could that be

because he had a mother
    and now I can see
you cannot have 2 people
    start a family tree

the same is true
    for creatures big and small
in species and pairs
    that swim, fly and crawl

I think that we came
    to this planet one night
into the galaxy
    on photons of light

an optical transmission
    of DNA codes
at the earth frequency
    and each night we reload

that could explain
    why after dusk we sleep
have light in our genes
    and programs we keep

wise men from afar
    what they thought was a star
I am the light of the world
    enlightening the dark

so let there be light
    as the Bible begins
God's aura delights
    as our light within

ONLY LOVE CAN KEEP

I want to transcend
   this consciousness
with 5 senses more
   or 5 senses less

to know if God
   can co-create
outside of love
   to separate

it cannot unite
   if everyone's right
with the things we hate
   we want to fight

in each other
    and in ourselves
where's the love
    that fear dispels

it must be hidden
    or buried deep
saved for favorites
    and sown to reap

at a later date
    and another week
unless my 5 senses
    only love can keep

HEART AND SOUL

O.M.G.
    look what's been done
life on earth
    our lessons begun

a game of chance
    supposed to be fun
to spiritually advance
    not supposed to be won

if I had known
    how the game was played
I'd have moved ahead
    not back or delayed

now I think I know
    each player's role
is to play the game
    with heart and soul

YOU AND ME

What is God
    but a way to see
inside itself
    through you and me

looking at worlds
    that we co-create
being its love
    as opposed to hate

note the key
    that love needs to be
is in the 2 words
    both 'you' and 'me'

I'LL KNOW MYSELF

I am finding
  it hard to believe
that life is an illusion
  and when we leave

we'll see the dream
  it will make more sense
to know the meaning
  it represents

why would I
  dream into being
all that I'm doing
  feeling and seeing

so I could know you
  and when I'm through
I'll know myself
  and know love too

I WONDER WHY

Now I'm here
   between earth and sky
on a rock in space
   and I wonder why

forget about how
   don't even try
the when is now
   and I wonder why

for love to show
   what it can do
in space and time
   through me and you

EACH OF US

How in the world
   could the earth be round
spheres in nature
   are only found

in an electron
   and as our sun
or a drop in a void
   they're the only ones

the moon and planets
   should look like rocks
unless they were liquid
   and started as drops

   drops from what
      and why not the same
   a fluid of elements
      from where they came

   became solids and gases
      and giant masses
   from heat and light
      consciousness flashes

   mind of God
      elements to dust
   God of mind
      in each of us

HERE, WHEN, AND HOW

Imagine two mirrors
    placed face to face
with you in the middle
    standing in place

infinite views
    forward and back
that do not exist
    a future and past

now move your arm
    the infinite changes
change your thought
    so unlimited arranges

the quantum field
    all connected to now
you in each moment
    here, when, and how

(and believe it or not
    the past changes too
all depending on
    the present you)

I LOVE TO BE

To my future self
   send me blessings through time
for our own good
   so we will align

so far ahead
   what do you find
before our decline
   please drop me a line

I'll send you a sign
   and tell you what hurts
what's assigned in your mind
   reality makes first

often in fear
   sometimes the worst
what you want to hear
   is how to reverse

what got you behind
  or you didn't deserve
to yourself be kind
  and you will preserve

self-love of mine
  in our thoughts and words
as we rewind
  and love is assured

because in every moment
  you are making me
your future self
  that I love to be

AFTERWORD

Please tell me how big is our universe?
As big as life and reality need it to be.

What is outside of it?
Gear up for this – only peace and love.

How far does our universe currently extend?
Farther than quiet healing can go, only farther.

Does it have a physical size?
Love has no size.

Please describe our universe.
Dear one – Is not each a temporary universe? The universe exists only for pieces of matter to each express love, only each reaches pieces of itself to know love.

Is our universe love?
Peace and love.

Is God love?
Not each love is God.

Is our universe God then?
Yes.

Which makes everything a part of God.
Right until fear opens the opposite name for love, making healing life a possibility.

For something to exist, its opposite also has to exist?
When the fear can realize a healing, it creates love.

And our universe expands?
Precisely.

What does it expand into?
Right into you.

So it expands inward rather than outward?
Farther than self-love can peacefully go.

Please explain more.
Patience and stillness are inward manifestations of God. Life appears to reality so that each time a fear realizes only healing peace and love, it opens the reality gates to manifest only life and what wishes the being makes.

And that is why you always stress healing fears near the heart when I ask how to manifest?
Life calls healing manifestations a miracle.

Is fear part of God or is it like a mirror just showing the opposite reflection of love?
All healing is of God, all fear is an illusion.

The universe is God and it is expanding inward?
Each time a healed fear has only realized itself and can face the illusion.

Why does God have aspects of an illusion?
If each of God's beings had no fear, peace and love would need balance. To each peace there requires non-peace, love requires non-love.

~Spirit message

POSTSCRIPT

These poems deal not only with life,
    but life and death;
love and end of life,
    meaning and afterlife.

Death is a part of life,
    giving life its passion
and love its compassion.

Life is limited.
    Love has no limits.

Love makes us eternal.

ABOUT THE AUTHOR

Poet, spirit
   dreamer, man
each life chose a purpose
   before it began

dreams seem real
   real seems like a dream
life is to heal
   unforgiven themes

within a book
   a thought and a prayer
love is perfect
   and expanding where

love is eternal
   life's internal affair
inside of you
   and All is there

what does it mean
   space with words in between
you are the author
   of all that is seen and unseen

www.ingramcontent.com/pod-product-compliance
Lightning Source LLC
Chambersburg PA
CBHW030554080526
44585CB00012B/371